DOLPHINS

by Josh Gregory

Children's Press®

An Imprint of Scholastic Inc.
New York   Toronto   London   Auckland   Sydney
Mexico City   New Delhi   Hong Kong
Danbury, Connecticut

Content Consultant
Dr. Stephen S. Ditchkoff
Professor of Wildlife Sciences
Auburn University
Auburn, Alabama

Photographs © 2012: age fotostock: 32 (Lisa Steiner), 35 (Ross
Armstrong); Alamy Images: cover (Arco Images GmbH), 19
(WaterFrame); AP Images/Kyodo: 39; Bob Italiano: 44 foreground,
45 foreground; Dreamstime/Tommy Schultz: 2 background, 3,
5 background, 44 background, 45 background; Getty Images/
Alexander Safonov: 28; iStockphoto/Alexander Novikov: 5 bottom,
40; Shutterstock, Inc.: 24 (Anna Segeren), 5 top, 31 (Miles Away
Photography), 7 (ShopArtGallery), 11 (Ulises Sepúlveda Déniz), 15
(york777); Superstock: 4, 8, 20, 23, 27, 36 (Minden Pictures),
1, 2 foreground, 12 (Tier und Naturfotogrfie);
The Image Works/Francois Gohier/V&W: 16.

Library of Congress Cataloging-in-Publication Data
Gregory, Josh.
  Dolphins/by Josh Gregory.
    p. cm.—(Nature's children)
  Includes bibliographical references and index.
  ISBN-13: 978-0-531-20900-4 (lib. bdg.)
    ISBN-10: 0-531-20900-8 (lib. bdg.)
  ISBN-13: 978-0-531-21075-8 (pbk.)
    ISBN-10: 0-531-21075-8 (pbk.)
  1. Dolphins—Juvenile literature. I. Title. II. Series.
  QL737.C432G75 2012
  599.53—dc23   2011031087

All rights reserved. Published in 2012 by Children's Press, an imprint
of Scholastic Inc.
Printed in the United States of America. 113
SCHOLASTIC, CHILDREN'S PRESS, and associated logos are
trademarks and/or registered trademarks of Scholastic Inc.

2 3 4 5 6 7 8 9 10 R 21 20 19 18 17 16 15 14 13

Dolphins

Class	Mammalia
Order	Cetacea
Families	Delphinidae and Platanistidae
Genera	21 genera (17 *Delphinidae* and 4 *Platanistidae*)
Species	37 species, including *Orcinus orca* (orca) and *Tursiops truncatus* (bottlenose dolphin)
World distribution	Worldwide in all oceans and seas, except for the Caspian and Aral Seas; river dolphins are found in South American and Asian rivers
Habitats	Oceans and rivers
Distinctive physical characteristics	Long, smooth, muscular bodies; wide tail flukes; needle-shaped teeth; beaklike mouths
Habits	Most live together in groups called pods; usually stay near the water's surface; never go completely to sleep
Diet	Mostly fish and invertebrates such as squid, lobster, and shrimp; some larger dolphins eat larger animals such as sharks

DOLPHINS

Contents

6 CHAPTER 1
Clever Creatures

18 CHAPTER 2
Survival at Sea

22 CHAPTER 3
Life in the Pod

30 CHAPTER 4
A Dolphin's Relatives

37 CHAPTER 5
Swimming into the Future

42 Words to Know

44 Habitat Map

46 Find Out More

47 Index

48 About the Author

Clever Creatures

Dolphins are some of the most intelligent and playful animals on Earth. They can learn many interesting tricks when in **captivity**. They even look friendly. The shape of their faces makes them look like they are always smiling.

Dolphins like to play games with the humans they meet. They are often seen **breaching** the waves as they follow along next to boats.

They might playfully knock off divers' goggles and snorkels. Sometimes dolphins will pick up boat anchors and move them. Dolphins also play with other sea creatures. They slide around on the noses of larger whales. They tease puffer fish to make them puff up. Sometimes they make toys out of sticks, seaweed, and other objects they find in the water.

Dolphins' playfulness and intelligence have made them some of the most beloved animals on Earth.

Where Do Dolphins Live?

Most dolphins live in oceans. Many of them will visit **freshwater** from time to time. But only five dolphin species live in freshwater all of the time. These dolphins live mainly in the long, wide rivers of Asia and South America. The Ganges in South Asia and the Amazon River in South America are both home to many river dolphins. They live far from their ocean cousins. They are often much smaller than ocean dolphins.

Ocean dolphins are found all over the world. Some live in warm areas near the **equator**. Others live in the ice-cold waters near the North and South Poles. Most dolphins do not swim very deep in the ocean waters. They live near the top so they can surface easily to breathe.

River dolphins have longer mouths than their ocean relatives.

9

Bottlenose and Common Dolphins

There are many different kinds of dolphins. But when most people think of dolphins, they think of bottlenose dolphins and common dolphins. These are the dolphins that people recognize from theme parks, zoos, and aquariums. They can be taught to do many tricks. Bottlenose dolphins are especially good at performing in shows for people. They are less afraid of people than common dolphins are. This makes it easier for them to get used to living in captivity.

But all dolphins are much happier living in the wild. They have more room to swim, and they get to live with other dolphins. Dolphins also live much longer in the wild than they do in captivity.

Special trainers work with captive dolphins to teach them new tricks.

Water Mammals

Many people look at dolphins and think that they might be fish. But dolphins are **mammals**. Humans and many other animals are also mammals. This means that dolphins have more in common with people than with fish. Mammals give birth to live babies. The babies drink milk from their mothers. Mammals are also warm-blooded. This means they don't need outside heat sources to keep their body temperatures at the right level. Cold-blooded animals such as lizards and snakes must spend time in the warm sun each day to keep their bodies from getting too cold.

All mammals have hair somewhere on their bodies. But hair is hard to find on most dolphins. Adult dolphins have a little bit of hair around their blowholes. Newborn dolphins have whiskers on the top half of their jaws. These whiskers fall out just a few days after the dolphins are born.

Grown dolphins have smooth, mostly hairless bodies.

What Do Dolphins Look Like?

One of a dolphin's most recognizable features is its **rostrum**. The rostrum is the beaklike mouth that all dolphins have. It contains many sharp, needlelike teeth. Bottlenose dolphins have between 80 and 100 teeth.

The front part of a dolphin's head is called the **melon**. The melon bulges out a little bit on most dolphins. A dolphin's blowhole is located behind the melon. Dolphins breathe through their blowholes.

A dolphin's tail fin is called a **fluke**. The fin on its back is known as the **dorsal fin**. Dolphins also have two flippers near the front of their bodies. These fins and flippers work together to help the dolphin swim and change direction.

Most dolphins are less than 10 feet (3 meters) long. Bottlenose dolphins grow as large as 12 feet (3.7 m) long and can weigh 1,100 pounds (500 kilograms). Males are usually a little larger than females.

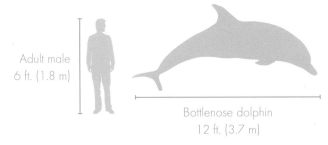

Adult male
6 ft. (1.8 m)

Bottlenose dolphin
12 ft. (3.7 m)

Dolphins' fins and flippers are very strong.

What Do Dolphins Eat?

All dolphins are **carnivorous**. This means that their diet consists entirely of other animals. Many dolphins eat fish. They also eat **invertebrates** such as shrimp, lobsters, crabs, and small squid. Larger dolphins such as orcas can eat even bigger prey. Some eat sharks, seals, polar bears, and other whales.

Dolphins can eat a lot of food. The average bottlenose dolphin eats between 15 and 30 pounds (6.8 to 13.6 kg) of food each day. Orcas can eat 10 to 20 times that amount. Dolphins do not chew their food. Instead, they swallow prey whole. Dolphins use their teeth to grab their food. Their needle-shaped teeth are not good at chewing, but they are very good at holding on to things.

FUN FACT! Breaching dolphins can launch themselves as far as 20 feet (6 m) above the water.

Orcas sometimes snatch young sea lions from beaches.

CHAPTER 2

Survival at Sea

Most ocean animals breathe by taking oxygen from the water around them. But dolphins breathe air, just as humans do. They must return to the water's surface to breathe. Dolphins can hold their breath much longer than people can. Dolphins usually breathe about once every 10 minutes.

Dolphins are excellent swimmers. Their smooth skin and long, muscular bodies allow them to move quickly and gracefully through the water. Bottlenose dolphins can swim as fast as 18.5 miles (30 kilometers) per hour. Common dolphins can swim even faster. The wide fluke at the end of a dolphin's tail provides power to move the dolphin through the water. The dorsal fin and the flippers help it turn.

Dolphins have lighter coloring on their bellies than on their backs. This helps them avoid **predators**. Predators looking from below will see a color that blends in with the brighter, sunlit ocean surface. Predators looking from above see a color that blends in with the darker ocean depths.

Spinner dolphins are known to travel in groups with bottlenose dolphins.

Echolocation

Most dolphins have good eyesight. But even with good vision, it is hard to see very far in ocean or river water. Dolphins use **echolocation** to help them find out what is ahead. A dolphin sends out high-pitched clicking sounds that bounce off objects and return to the dolphin. These sound waves are created in and directed by the dolphin's melon. The returning sounds are absorbed by the dolphin's lower jaw. **Nerves** behind the jaw transfer the information to the dolphin's brain.

The dolphin can use information from echolocation to figure out how far away something is. It can then use this information to avoid obstacles and find prey. Echolocation can also be used to stun fish that the dolphin wants to eat.

Echolocation tells dolphins about the size, shape, and speed of their prey.

CHAPTER 3

Life in the Pod

Most dolphins live together in groups called **pods**. Some pods are as small as two or three dolphins. Others contain dozens of dolphins. Sometimes pods join together to form even larger groups. These groups can grow to include several thousand dolphins at a time. Dolphins help other members of their pod find food. They also warn each other about dangers and help protect each other from predators.

Some dolphins stay in the same pod their whole lives. They live with their mothers and other relatives. Other dolphins form new pods with dolphins their own age. Smaller pods usually live in the shallow water near a shoreline. Larger pods usually live farther out into the ocean.

Not every dolphin species lives in pods. Amazon River dolphins live by themselves. They do not rely on each other to help find food or avoid threats.

Some dolphins join and leave several pods throughout their lives.

Dolphin Babies

Dolphins give birth to one baby at a time. They **reproduce** once every two to five years. A baby dolphin is called a **calf**. Calves are born live instead of hatching from eggs. They can swim as soon as they are born. Calves are raised by their mothers and other female dolphins in the pod. Mother dolphins keep their calves close. For the first months of their lives, calves only drink milk from their mothers. They start learning to hunt after a few months, but they continue drinking milk until they are about a year and a half old.

Calves and mothers often go without sleep for more than a month after the baby is born. Even fully grown dolphins do not sleep like people do. Dolphins sleep with one eye open. Only one side of a dolphin's brain sleeps at a time. A dolphin stays partly awake to swim to the surface and breathe.

Baby dolphins are usually born tail first.

Dolphin Talk

Dolphins have many ways of communicating with each other. This helps them work together to hunt for food, avoid danger, and even play. They can make more than 2,000 different sounds, including whistles, clicks, and barks. Some scientists believe that these sounds form a language like the ones humans use. Some dolphins have special sounds that they use to identify themselves. These sounds are like names the dolphins give themselves.

Dolphins also communicate using their bodies. They can slap their tails on the surface of the water to indicate danger or show where something is. They rub fins with each other as a greeting. Sometimes they swim next to each other while touching fins, just as humans hold hands. They often roll over onto their backs in order to show **submission** to other dolphins.

Scientists use special equipment to listen to dolphin sounds and learn more about how dolphins communicate.

Family Meals

Most dolphins work together with their pods to hunt for food. They have several tricks that they use to capture prey. Sometimes a pod will surround a **school** of fish. Then members of the pod will take turns charging into the center of the school and snatching fish to eat. Other times, the pod will herd its prey into the shallow waters near the shore. This makes it harder for the prey to escape. Dolphins sometimes hit fish with their tails to stun them. Sometimes they even bat the fish right out of the water. They can also use echolocation to stun prey.

Dolphins are often willing to travel very far to find the foods they like best. Pods have been known to travel hundreds of miles as they hunt.

FUN FACT! Dolphins can recognize each other by the shapes of their dorsal fins just as well as people recognize each other's faces.

Dolphin pods can easily outsmart schools of smaller fish.

CHAPTER 4

A Dolphin's Relatives

Dolphins are a type of **cetacean**, or whale. They belong to a group known as the toothed whales. Other types of toothed whales include porpoises, sperm whales, and beluga whales. Unlike other whales, toothed whales have teeth and only one blowhole. Other whales have two blowholes.

There are two **families** of dolphins. Ocean dolphins belong to the family Delphinidae. River dolphins belong to the family Platanistidae. The two families combined have a total of 37 dolphin species. Six of those species are usually referred to as whales instead of dolphins. Some dolphin species are mistakenly referred to as porpoises. But true porpoises do not have a dolphin's long rostrum or needlelike teeth. Instead, they have shorter snouts and flat teeth.

Belugas are toothed whales, but they are not dolphins.

Different Dolphins

Bottlenose and common dolphins are the most familiar dolphin species. But other dolphin species are just as interesting. Another well-known species is the orca. Orcas are also called killer whales. They are the largest dolphin species. They can grow to be 30 feet (9 m) long and weigh up to 12,000 pounds (5,443 kg). They also live up to 90 years, which is much longer than most dolphins live. Smaller dolphins only live about 15 years on average.

The spinner dolphin gets its name from its ability to spin in the air as it breaches. The spinner can twirl all the way around up to four times. This dolphin typically grows to be about 7 feet (2 m) long.

Risso's dolphins are known for playing rough. They often play by slamming into each other. Many of them are covered in scars from playing so hard. They usually grow to around 10 feet (3 m) long.

Risso's dolphins do not have the long rostrums that many other dolphin species have.

Even More Dolphins

Amazon river dolphins often live alone instead of traveling in pods. If they do form pods, they are usually made up of very few dolphins. Some scientists believe that they have the best echolocation abilities of any dolphin species. Amazon river dolphins are also called boto. Like most other dolphins, they are friendly to humans.

The smallest dolphin species is the rare Hector's dolphin of New Zealand. Hector's dolphins grow to be about 4 feet (1.2 m) long and weigh about 110 pounds (50 kg). There are only about 7,400 of these small dolphins living today.

Dolphins have been on Earth for a very long time. Scientists have discovered dolphin fossils that date back as far as 23.8 million years ago. Not all of the dolphin species that existed in the past still live today. Some species have gone **extinct**.

Hector's dolphin was first discovered in 1869.

CHAPTER 5

Swimming into the Future

Dolphins do not always have easy lives. Human activities are the biggest threat to dolphin species everywhere. One of the largest problems is **pollution**. Humans often dump trash and harmful chemicals into the ocean and other bodies of water. Smaller fish sometimes eat the trash and chemicals. These fish become poisonous. Dolphins get sick when they eat them. All water systems on Earth are connected, from the smallest pond to the biggest ocean. This means that all water pollution can eventually affect dolphins and other ocean life.

Many dolphins live in areas where there is a lot of human activity.

Threats from Fishers

Pollution isn't the only human threat to dolphins. Some people hunt dolphins for food. They kill thousands of dolphins every year. It is even more common for dolphins to be killed accidentally by fishers who are trying to catch shrimp, swordfish, and other ocean animals commonly eaten by humans. Thousands of dolphins are caught in these fishers' nets each year. Tuna fishers were once responsible for an especially large number of dolphin deaths. New laws and special nets have helped to lower the number of these accidents.

Fishing can also harm dolphins in less direct ways. In some parts of the world, fishers are allowed to catch as many fish as they want. This has lowered the populations of some species, leaving less food for dolphins. Fishing boats themselves can make life hard for dolphins. Vibrations from their engines can make it difficult for dolphins to use echolocation.

Fishers must be careful to avoid catching dolphins in their nets.

Protecting Dolphins

Many governments and organizations around the world are working to protect dolphins. In 1972, the United States government passed the Marine Mammal Protection Act. This law makes it illegal for people to touch, feed, or bother any dolphins or other whales living in the wild.

Conservation organizations work to help dolphins by researching how and why dolphins get caught in fishing nets. They use this information to find new ways of preventing dolphins from getting accidentally captured or injured by these nets.

Zoos and aquariums sometimes help dolphins by rescuing injured dolphins from areas along the coast. They help heal these dolphins and then release them back into the ocean.

Dolphins will have a long and healthy future if people around the world work to prevent pollution and other threats.

If we work to prevent pollution, dolphins will be our friends for many years to come.

Words to Know

breaching (BREECH-ing) — rising to the water's surface to breathe

calf (KAF) — the young of several large species of animals, such as dolphins, cows, and seals

captivity (kap-TIV-i-tee) — the condition of being held or trapped by people

carnivorous (kar-NIV-ur-uhs) — having meat as a regular part of the diet

cetacean (si-TAY-shuhn) — water-dwelling mammals, including all whale species

conservation (kon-sur-VAY-shun) — the act of protecting an environment and the living things in it

dorsal fin (DOR-suhl FIN) — the fin located on the back of many marine animals, such as dolphins and sharks

echolocation (eh-koh-loh-KAY-shuhn) — process of using sound waves to locate the position of objects in the water

equator (i-KWAY-tur) — an imaginary line around the middle of Earth that is an equal distance from the North and South Poles

extinct (ik-STINGKT) — no longer found alive

families (FAM-uh-leez) — groups of living things that are related to each other

fluke (FLOOK) — part of the tail of a sea creature such as a whale or dolphin

freshwater (FRESH-wah-tur) — water that does not contain salt

invertebrates (in-VUR-tuh-brits) — animals without a backbone

mammals (MAM-uhlz) — warm-blooded animals that have hair or fur and usually give birth to live young

melon (MEL-uhn) — the front part of a dolphin's head

nerves (NURVZ) — the threads that send messages between the brain and other parts of the body to move and feel

pods (PAHDZ) — groups of certain kinds of sea animals, such as dolphins and other whales

pollution (puh-LOO-shuhn) — harmful materials that damage or contaminate the air, water, and soil

predators (PREH-duh-turz) — animals that live by hunting other animals for food

reproduce (ree-pruh-DOOS) — to produce offspring or individuals of the same kind

rostrum (RAH-strum) — the beaklike mouth of a dolphin

school (SKOOL) — a group of fish or other sea creatures swimming or feeding together

submission (sub-MISH-uhn) — giving in to the control or authority of someone or something

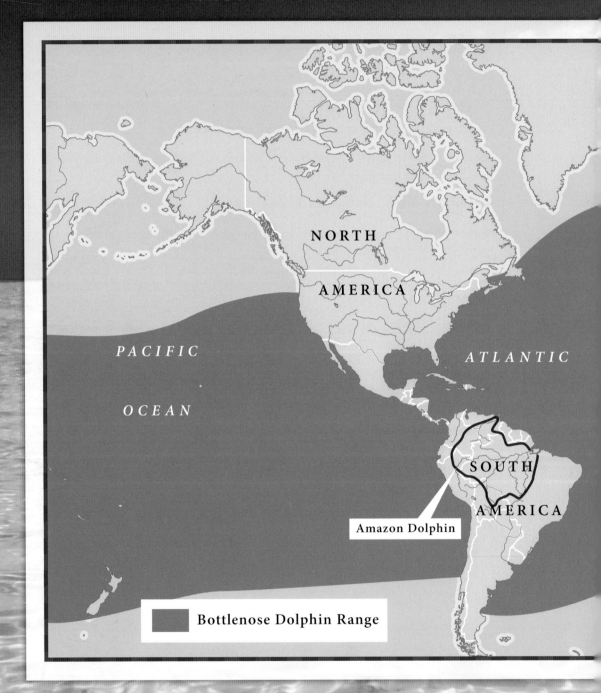

NORTH

AMERICA

PACIFIC

OCEAN

ATLANTIC

SOUTH

AMERICA

Amazon Dolphin

Bottlenose Dolphin Range

ARCTIC OCEAN

EUROPE

ASIA

AFRICA

PACIFIC OCEAN

OCEAN

INDIAN OCEAN

Ganges Dolphin

AUSTRALIA

Find Out More

Books

Carney, Elizabeth. *National Geographic Kids Everything Dolphins*. Washington, DC: National Geographic Society, 2012.

Nicklin, Flip, and Linda Nicklin. *Face to Face with Dolphins*. Washington, DC: National Geographic, 2007.

Rizzo, Johnna. *Oceans*. Washington, DC: National Geographic, 2010.

Web Sites

San Diego Zoo—Animal Bytes: Dolphin
www.sandiegozoo.org/animalbytes/t-dolphin.html
Learn interesting facts and look at pictures of dolphins in the wild.

WWF—Whales and Dolphins
www.worldwildlife.org/species/finder/cetaceans/whalesanddolphins.html
Learn about whale and dolphin species that are in danger of dying out.

Visit this Scholastic web site for more information on dolphins:
www.factsfornow.scholastic.com

Index

aquariums, 10, 41

babies. See calves.
beluga whales, 30, *31*
births, 13, 25
blowholes, 13, 14, 30
body temperatures, 13
bottlenose dolphins, 10, 14, 17, 18, 33
brains, 21, 25
breaching, 6, 17, 33
breathing, 9, 14, 18, 25

calves, 13, *24*, 25
captivity, 6, 10, *11*, 41
cetaceans, 30
colors, 18
common dolphins, 10, 18, 33
communication, 22, 26, *27*
conservation, 38, *39*, 41

Delphinidae family, 30
dorsal fins, 14, 18, 29

echolocation, *20*, 21, 29, 34, 38
extinction, 34
eyes, 21, 25

females, 13, 14, 22, 25
fins, 14, *15*, 18, 26, 29
fishing nets, 38, *39*, 41
flippers, 14, *15*, 18
flukes, 14, 18, *24*, 26, 29

food. *See* prey.
fossils, 34
freshwater, 9

groups. *See* pods.

habitats, 9, 22, *36*
hair, *12*, 13
Hector's dolphins, 34, *35*
hunting, 21, 25, 26, *28*, 29, 38

intelligence, 6, *7*, *28*, 29

jaws, 13, 21

killer whales. *See* orcas.

laws, 38, 41
life spans, 10, 33

males, 14
Marine Mammal Protection Act (1972), 41
melon, 14, 21
milk, 13, 25

names, 26, 33
nerves, 21

orcas, *16*, 17, 33

people, 10, *11*, 13, 18, 34, *36*, 37, 38, *39*, *40*, 41

(Index continued)

Platanistidae family, 30
playing, 6, 26, 33
pods, 22, *23*, 25, *28*, 29, 34
pollution, 37, 38, 41
populations, 38
porpoises, 30
predators, 18, 22, 38
prey, *16*, 17, 21, 22, 26, *28*, 29, 37, 38

Risso's dolphins, *32*, 33
river dolphins, *8*, 9, 22, 30, 34
rostrums, 14, 30, *32*

scientists, 26, *27*, 34
senses, 21
sizes, 9, 14, *14*, 33, 34
skin, *12*, 18
sleeping, 25

snouts. *See* rostrums.
sounds, 21, 26
speeds, 18
spinner dolphins, *19*, 33
submission, 26
swimming, 9, 10, 14, 18, 25, 26

tail fins. *See* flukes.
teeth, 14, 17, 30
toothed whales, 30
travel, 29
tricks, 6, 10, *11*, 29

weight, 14, 33, 34
whales, 6, 17, 30, *31*, 41
whiskers, 13

zoos, 10, 41

About the Author

Josh Gregory writes and edits books for kids. He lives in Chicago, Illinois.